MIDDLE
AGING WITHOUT GRACE

POEMS BY
JANET PITLER

MIDDLE AGE MELT
©2022 by Janet Pitler
Norfolk, Virginia

ISBN:
978-1-953024-98-5

Table Of Contents

ACKNOWLEDGEMENTS

I was told I needed an acknowledgement page.

I acknowledge that I'm old. I acknowledge that unwrapped package; that wonderfully young, physically adept, naively unaware, unwrinkled, unsuspecting persona that segued into the opposite... the fodder for this book

I acknowledge my amazingly tolerant husband, Steve, who still thinks I am that unwrapped package...he is the kindest, most understanding and supportive, lovely person I know. Sorry people, there's more. If you made it through this far and haven't hurled, you might want to grab a bucket and force yourself to read on.

Steve, thank you for growing old with me and putting up with my hormonal outrages, lack of confidence and toot scoots. And, my children, Damon, Evan, and Amy (Damon's beautiful wife), and my grandchildren, Theodora, Veronica, Logan and Lucinda. You're the beginning of my end and you're the reason I am going out with a smile.

PROLOGUE

We were young.
We were healthy.
We were happy.
We were unaware.
That
Menopausal Maladies
and
Man's Milllusions
Would become the norm.

MIDDLE AGE
AND THUS, IT BEGINS

Assessed and Redressed

I'd reached the age of 50
Wasn't happy, wasn't not.
Felt a nagging in my mindset:
"Check the body! Is it shot?"

I'd had some daily soreness,
Knew I'd slowed down just a bit.
So I made a quick assessment,
Checked to see if I was fit.

Not too "aged" nor too caving
Muscle mass seemed fairly tight...
My skin was not too saggy
And I still retained my height.

But I knew my time was coming
Not too far there down the block.
Was aware I had to face it:
I could not outrun the clock.

I'd finally reached that milestone
Knew I'd turned that dreadful page,
Knee deep in aging hormones,
Up to my neck in middle age.

About Those Wings!

Wings are works of wonder
Meant for soaring high aloft.
I always pictured feathers
White and flawless, smooth and soft.

The wings I saw were stately
Wide and wonderful they were.
Their elegance was simple
Quite so lovely ... "haute couture."

The wings I always wanted
That first moment from the start
Were the wings I always pictured
In my dreams and in my heart.

With dreams one must be wary
Quite selective, clearly smart
Making sure what one's requesting
Is most surely à la carte.

Thus, the day I finally noticed
Having turned and mirrored in
I saw aging arms unfettered,
Fallen low, to my chagrin.

My wings were not the trim ones
Sleek and lovely they were not.
They crushed the lofty vision
That my mind had clearly sought.

Epiphany emerging,
Eyes widening at the sight
Saw that nature's sense of humor
Preferred appendage blight.

Consolidation

I've tried to figure how
My knees and thighs got
meshed.
All that comes to mind now's:
My muscles got out-fleshed.

Where once I had two
kneecaps
So firmly well defined
There lies a conformation
Where folds of skin entwine.

The muscle tone that dazzled
From hip straight down to
knee
Has slipped with gravitation
To a distant memory.

Just below my middle body
Where that firmness reigned
supreme
The collagen formations
Are nowhere to be seen.

Since I still have an ego
And a shred of self-respect
I'll ensure my body's covered
From my knees up to my neck.

Mind Game

Was I heading to the bathroom
Or reaching for my coat?
Had I meant to call my cousin
Or to search for the remote?

Was I heading to the kitchen
When I was walking down the
hall
Or going to my bedroom
As I walked into a wall?

Did I pay the monthly phone bill?
Was that the mortgage check I
sent?

Did I take my little pink pill?
Was it the blue one that I meant?

Perhaps my mind has left me
Gone to find a better place...
The thoughts that used to run
free
Seem so easily erased.

It appears the complication
Is the one I can't regret.
I've forgotten to remember
That I forgot that I forget.

High School Reunion

Ten years had passed; they'd gone so fast
I'd somehow passed the time.
I'd held my own, my ego grown...
Still clearly in my prime.

So, when I saw that letter,
Its logo rising proud,
I knew at my reunion
I'd stand out in the crowd.

That night I'd shown, I had
come home.
The years had taught me how.
I relished all the lavish praise.
My time was here and now.

I vowed my next reunion I'd
Look better, laissez-faire...
Walk in, be thin, be full of pride
With head so dark and full of hair.

And that I did, looked just the same,
My body'd held and still looked fine,
But knew more years would change the game...
That time would rudely cross the line.

One day not too much later,
I noticed things weren't going right.
Time had been less friendly...
I'd aged ten years just overnight.

So much for class reunions.
The thought just makes me numb.
Mature with class. Forget the past.
I'll face my aging with aplomb.

THEN, DISINTEGRATES FURTHER

Children

We once had dreams of offspring
Fulfilled quite long ago,
The creation of a new wing
Of a family that would grow.

But we never once envisioned
How fast the years would go,
How quickly our own children
Would get older and then sow.

There's nothing wrong with children.
They are marvelous when planned.
But before you're over sixty,
That noun should not begin with "grand."

Addressing PMS'ing

I was used to PMS'ing,
To that monthly, hateful mess,
But now I'm menopausal
With a different kind of stress.

I feel lots of heavy bloating
Because subtle it is not.
I've had to raise my pants size,
Loose the hook another notch.

Body's moisture always flowing,
Feeling clammy with each
breath
Exponentially expanding,
Breaking out into a sweat!

That monthly thing had been
there
Always causing me duress,
But since I've got this new
"thing"
I've done nothing but regress.

Now I'm living with a waistband
That is wider than before.
And my temperature keeps
rising
Sending sweat out through each
pore.

My body grabbed this new
thing,
Leaving PMS behind,
Hormones are always fighting,
Always messing with my mind.

I now understand revision.
PMS was just a game,
Menopause is a derision.
Only here to screw my brain

Adherence

I used to eat my calories
By the bushel and the pound.
When I was young and trimmer
They never hung around.

I'd gorge myself with burgers
Shakes and fries and onion rings.
I'd eat whatever didn't move.
I'd chew on anything.

Sodas were my mainstay
Graduating on to beer.
I drank them both with pizza.
Still, the pounds did not adhere.

And when I drank my coffee
Always full of heavy cream,
I'd load it up with sugar
And then inhale the steam.

Now time has taken over
And has slowed my system down.
Those fats that never fazed me
Have begun to stick around.

Though I've switched from beer and pizza,
And become a low-cal jock,
My ever-growing fat cells
Are in a state of overstock.

Blemish

Lifts and lasers are my
friends
But the process
never ends.
With the facial
wear and tear
It will always need
repair.

Thus, as aging cells
convene,
They continue their routine,
With their mission to complete:
"Let's make firmness obsolete!"

All the younger cells they meet
Are more subtle and discreet
As the havoc they create
Keeps them ready to mutate.

So, as I rubbed and as I
cleaned,
As I toned and then I creamed
All the softly, lifted skin
From my forehead to my chin,

I was fully unaware
  Those younger cells
    had left their lair.
      They had joined and
      multiplied
    Found a place they
    could reside.

  With their work
    completely done
  Having had a day of fun
They then waited through the
night
To see what happened at first
light.

They must have shivered with
delight
When I awoke and saw the
blight…
That with a shudder and a sigh,
I'd had to welcome my third
eye.

But for the Butt

For all those times I had to sit
There was no need for perfect fit,
Just something classy, lots of style,
To rest my feet and chill a while.

My butt was firm. It felt so tight.
Could sit, feel comfort all the night.
But things have changed, it seems of late
Before I sit . . . I hesitate.

I seek a soft and spacious place
To seat my butt with style and grace.
Seems things have spread beyond repair.
It's tough to find a cushy chair.

Alas, the scourge of middle age
Has now become an anal stage:
I need to prove that I can sit
Where my fat butt will never fit.

Conversating

As children, conversations
Weren't considered in that vein.
Just communications...
No thought from brain to brain.

And, then through our progression
From playground into school,
A new mindset would take over,
But with concepts miniscule.

Let's skip now to the stage
Where hormones make their move
As conversations aren't important
And connections find their groove.

There's way much less of talking
As passion makes its way
Exploring all the venues
Conversations go away.

Relationships develop.
Connections become clear.
And then with maturation,
Conversations reappear.

The topics, then of marriage,
Later houses, kids abound
Evolving into subjects
After kids are not around.

Then topics seem to segue into
Sources of our pain,
Of our aging bodies
And the functions that remain.

Though we're thankful just to be here
Still around in our domain
Our conversations are now centered
On what's left of our poor brain.

Cute

"Cute" is for small babies
Kittens, puppies and that lot.
It's also used for toddlers
With their noses full of snot.

It's used for kids with freckles
With pug noses and wild hair.
And often for a photo
Of a monkey in a chair.

I used that term quite often
As those cuties passed me by
And felt the joy it gave me.
Never had to wonder why.

I remember seeing ladies
Somewhat crinkled with old age
Holding hands with their beloveds
Who had also reached that stage.

I smiled as my thoughts filled me
With the nicest kind of bliss.
They looked so sweet and happy…
It seemed nothing was amiss.

I remember very clearly
Having seen them many times
And never once envisioned
Even though there were some signs

That one day someone would see
Me in that very clear same vein…
That "cuteness" would define me
And I'd hear that same refrain.

Those very words I'd spoken
As I passed those couples by
Would come back and bite my ego
Right there just above my thigh.

Dots, Spots Then Splotch

The splatter of small freckles
Were always thought quite cute.
They gave a sense of freshness
That exuded bliss of youth.

Add a smile and sense of humor
And then naivite
Combined with youthful outlook
A touch of joy came into play.

But, adding too much sunshine
And loading on some age
Those freckles would start
spreading
Way too fast and hard to
gauge.

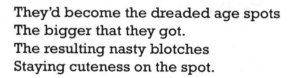

And then they'd start connecting
In a very subtle way
So their movement, never noticed
Meant no one'd see them stray.

They'd become the dreaded age spots
The bigger that they got.
The resulting nasty blotches
Staying cuteness on the spot.

When we were so much younger
And cute, and fun and hot,
We missed the mangled masses
Evolving splotch to splotch.

So, since choice is not an option
With our jig-sawed, spot-stained face
We'll just have to grin and bear it
As we watch them interlace.

Eking Creaking

My body started talking,
Speaking crackles, speaking creaks.
Heard the noise as I was walking,
There were loud and endless squeaks.

Knew the years had aged my body,
Left no tone, nor strength nor grace.
I was left with something shoddy
Somewhat cracked, somewhat defaced.

Those daily, noisy movements
From this sorry aged physique
Have clearly, sadly proven
That my body's past its peak.

Excess Baggage

Just a quarter of an inch
Sitting there below my eyes
There looms some excess baggage
I would like to neutralize.

I did not request dark circles,
Not the heavy, sagging style.
If I had wanted baggage
I'd have ordered crocodile!

Gray Hair Elsewhere

I had long ago
accepted
Scattered gray hairs
on my head,
I could wake and
face them daily
With no remorse
and without dread.

I continued with
my life's plan,
Scheduled work along
with play,
Until that fateful
morning
When that life plan went
astray:

With my foot in
downward motion
Heading straight into my shorts,
My eyes spied a little light thing
And my mind said to" abort."

I slowed, though still in motion,
Geared my move down to a
stop,
And looked a bit more closely
At my body's middle mop.

Amid the dark and tangled
Clearly present motley curls
There rose a gray intruder
Standing tall, it stood unfurled.

I then lost a couple heartbeats
Left my breath behind a mile
And, while staring, lost my
mindset
    Asked if life was still
    worthwhile.

        In that moment, I stopped
        thinking
    Just reached down and pulled
it out!
    So it was gone. I could move on
Without fear and with no doubt.

But then one day I noticed
Something strange there on
my face:
        It stood there in my
        eyebrow,
        A touch of gray I
should erase.

When I looked a bit more
closely
And saw an eyelash just as light,
I knew grays would keep on
coming,
Multiply both day and night

So I took a long and deep breath,
Thought a minute more or so…
Gray hair was there. It sure beat
bare.
I'd accept the status quo.

Hips and Knees

New hips, new knees, I beg for these
All day and through each night.
I go to sleep with hopes so deep
My prayers will turn out right.

As daylight comes, while still in bed
I begin to fight the fight.
I do so with a touch of dread…
My hips are locked up tight.

I try to move but once more prove
Some wishes don't come true.
Appears my knees, still stuck in "freeze,"
Will surely not come through…

As I never know which knee will go
I wait a moment more.
And hope my feet, a pair complete,
Are first to hit the floor.

Sometimes that doesn't happen.
They're more often stuck than not.
Though I'm aware I'll need repair
I give it one more shot.

Shift my right leg just a little,
Test its limits as it moves,
Edge my body to the bedside…
Hope the pain I feel improves.

As my left leg joins my right,
And thoughts of pain run through my head…
With my hips still locked up tight
I somehow make it out of bed.

I go to take my pain pills
Cuss a little, face my plight,
See the doctors, pay their huge bills
And attempt to sleep at night.

Then once again each morning
I'll begin to raise my head
Ignore my body's warning…
Inch my way out of the bed.

Middle Age Melt

The excess on my face
Seeking out an empty space
Cascaded down my neck
Into a wrinkled, sagging wreck.

The melting that ensued
Made the rest become unglued
Proceeding without stress
Pushing southward on my chest.

With nowhere else to go
It continued down below
To take my stomach's place
Which had no time to brace.

Then my belly found its space
Way too far below my waist
Hitting squarely on my thighs
Where now my belly button lies.

My once round and youthful knees
Though faint from all that stress
Still felt they could appease
All the crumpled, falling mess.

But then my calves gave in
And said, "Oh, what the heck!
Let's hold up what we can!
We'll never fix this wreck!"

So as my ankles were encroached
They knew they should be coached
In their hope to catch the rest
Without being overstressed.

But when my ankles failed,
Their poor ligaments assailed,
My overstressed and flattish feet
Found strength, would not retreat!

They took a fearless stance
As they watched the bulk advance,
Aware that even with synapse
My legs could still collapse.

So, they stayed and held their ground
Planned to duel from round to round
Knowing Middle Age Melt
Always fights below the belt.

Protuberances

Thank heavens I'm still hearing.
My ears are working well.
My nose is just as happy.
I still have a sense of smell.

However, I have noticed
When checking out my face
That something is quite different...
Something out of place...

The symmetry that'd been there,
The equilibrium that I'd known
Was no longer in position
My ears had lost some tone.

They had gotten longer...
No respect for symmetry
The drooping lobes submitting
To years of gravity

That my nose had dipped a little,
Its perkiness had gone.
And, it seemed a whole lot bigger
Also, sadly, very long.

The reflection I'm now seeing
Wasn't what I thought it'd be.
I'd accepted skin was sagging
Touched with wrinkles full of glee.

But, the frightening combination
Of my drooping ears and nose
Has confirmed for generations
That getting older really blows.

Navigation

I remember driving safely
In sync with other cars
With traffic moving smoothly
Though, I'd stopped at several bars.

The center lines were stable
My mind and vision clear
Obeying all the signals
As each one would appear.

But, lately I have noticed
As my sight and reflex wane
I don't see those lines and signals
Regardless how I strain.

The steering wheel's much higher.
I've had to raise my seat a bit
And my swerving seems to anger
All the people that I hit.

It would be so very
simple
If all those people
stayed aware.
The most important rule of
driving
Is to "Avoid those with
gray hair!"

Question of Digestion

I was sitting down, relaxing
When I heard my body speak.
My stomach started talking
And it sounded pretty bleak:

"It's a question of digestion,"
Said my stomach to my brain.
"Are you really going to eat that
Or do you think you could refrain?

"I haven't had a chance yet
To digest what's sitting here,
What's swirling in the acid
Mixed with sausages and beer.

"Could you hold off just a second?
Slow it down and take a breath?
Could you eat less grease and junk food
And stop feeding me to death!

"All the years you've made the choices,
Never stopping once to think.
You've been eating what you want to . . .
I am not the kitchen sink!

"When I spoke to operations
All the organs there agreed,
You can still do all the thinking,
But must stop the food stampede.

"We'll agree to work together,
Decrease the gas, turn down the heat,
But you must keep your end in order
Or learn new meanings for repeat!"

?Picasso?

I spent years on reparations
Owing so much to my face,
Never made the calculations,
Just fixed things case by case.

Lines had formed with no
conception
Of how wide or of how deep
They should make each cruel
depression
With no regard for its upkeep.

Still I kept up with the damage
Until I felt my work was done,
Felt comfortable and happy
That my face and I were one.

Facial features were familiar
When viewed each passing day,
But the lines continued forming
Slightly hidden, held at bay.

Time played its game while
cheating,
Let me forget that it's a clock
As it quietly kept eating
All the collagen I've got.

Let's just say that time was subtle
Working slowly from the start
Then climaxed when my
reflection
Revealed the worst of modern art.

Regretting Sweating

I swear I know I'm melting
My thermostat's on high.
I've been this way for months now
And think I've figured why.

It's this menopausal mayhem
Causing me to go amuck,
The barrage of faulty signals
With which my body's gotten stuck.

Since I no longer "glisten"
But now sweat from head to toe
And the moisture keeps on building
In a never-ending flow,

I've had to change my schedules
Put my fashion sense on hold
Find some water-proven makeup,
Hope this mess can be controlled.

But the cause is just a moot point.
It's the cure that's paramount.
There must be a good solution…
A reprieve might even count!

Unless my body listens
And turns off its flowing spout
I'll be wearing sweats and
headbands
Until I cool off or just wash out!

The Scoop On Poop

As potty-training children
We were awarded with applause.
Each time we made a nice poop
We were rewarded without pause.

Each day we learned that pooping
Could be a pleasant thing.
No need for some regrouping...
Our bum could even sing.

When we got a little older
As little kids, it was a breeze.
We even got much bolder
And held it in with just a squeeze.

Potty-training was forgotten,
As an important part of youth.
Our growth had simply gotten
Where thoughts of pooping were uncouth.

But as we've gotten older
So glad to wake each day...
Our poops have gotten colder.
And our bowels have gone astray.

Now sitting on our buttocks
Our patience growing thin
Our intestines still in deadlock
Feeling poop up to our chin.

We're waiting there surrounded
Feel the silence closing in.
Where applause had once abounded
There was nothing but chagrin.

Topographic Errors

The layout of my body
Isn't what it used to be.
Those high and shapely mountains
Have succombed to gravity.

They're more akin to hillocks
With some deeply sliding slopes.
And the valley that defined me
Has lost its lust for gropes.

My skin once full of thickness,
Had shown some blueish veins,
But, now's a map of rivers
Which very clearly drain

Into my lower body
Where my muscles are now skewed
Along with all the sinew
That my body has eschewed.

Physiology has screwed me
With the passing of its time
And has left me with a layout
Topographically maligned.

Toot Scoot

I've learned to do the Toot Scoot
Though it doesn't make me proud.
It'll never be the Mute Scoot
For it only plays out loud.

I've done it in an airplane
Where the noise was safely drowned.
I've done it in a ballroom
Where the music blocked the sound.

The important steps are easy
As I'm propelled across the floor,
To the bathroom, to the right spot
With hope I make it through the door.

Maturation Saturation

Couldn't wait to get there
To develop boobs and hips.
To finally see some new hair
Growing there on my ellipse.

I couldn't wait for high school
To prove that I had grown…
Matured and with my new cool
Could go forward on my own.

Ah, college was a given
Had waited there for me.
To know I'd found my rhythm
Found the realm of ecstasy.

As I sped through all those years
Where "matured me" had to be
Keeping up with all my peers
With no thought that agony

Would attack my aging main
frame
Saturating every cell
Going right into the endgame
Into a special kind of hell.

Those boobs and hips I prayed for
The height that I had gained
Were attracted to the ground
floor
Where gravity explained:

"Maturation gauged its stages
Never thinking to explain
I'd spend my final pages…
Saturated with no drain."

REPAIRING DISREPAIR

Body Armor

When I ask for lingerie
The staffs of stores wherein I shop
Try to breathe, then kneel and pray
Begin to dig and search nonstop.

What they seek to fit me now
Is built with lifts and yards of stuff,
But they'll find it! Yes, they vow,
Once they've seen me in the buff.

Those days of silk and fitted lace
Part of my youthful, naïve past
Have now quite simply been erased
With things that fit my big fat ass.

Bonding Of The Blonding

Have you noticed when you're gathered
With the over-fifty lot,
The bulk of all the women are
More often blonde than not?

They know that men see blonde hair
 As their fountain, source of youth.
They see that coloration
As their version of the truth.

Most guys are just there searching
For a batch of new recruits
While most women are just thankful
To have covered their gray roots.

Cavity Depravity

My teeth were strong, not perfect,
But they had their simple grace.
Their job was sweet and simple:
Help put a smile upon my face.

When just a kid, things worked quite well,
A set of teeth had come and gone.
The second set was in its place,
But after that some things went wrong.

Though I had flossed and daily brushed,
Decay began to grow and build.
My dentist worked to get me straight,
He cleaned and drilled, and promptly filled.

With time this stayed the pattern,
He repaired from tooth to tooth.
But cavities got bigger...
Sensed I'd lost the shield of youth.

More fillings joined with fillings,
And saw expansion as their goal.
My dentist sold the need for crowns,
That priceless porcelain had a role.

Then tooth by tooth, he left his mark,
Replacing darkened, weakened space.
And with each crown, he gained some ground.
Left no decay, not one small trace.

Those efforts though so noble
Building strength and building grace
Couldn't stop my gums' recession...
Determined now to win the race.

The only smile that's brighter now
Has graced another doctor's face.
I'm still perplexed and don't know how
A periodontist took his place.

Cover The Gray Day

As I looked into the mirror
Gazing bravely straight therein
Saw a face much "slightly older,"
It wasn't what it'd been.

My eyes moved slowly upward
Starting just below my chin
From cheek to cheek, then to my nose,
Hesitating, with chagrin.

Checked out the scraggy eyebrows,
Deepened furrows etched above,
Then reached my thinning hairline
Where my gaze abruptly froze.

What I saw there was a
gray tract,
Such a blatant, ugly
line…
Had no idea how it got
there,
It must have been benign.

When I finally recovered
From the fact that what I'd
seen
Was not a dull illusion
But a blight, a scourge,
obscene.

I sighed and gathered courage,
Feeling angered, still aghast.
I faced my cover-gray day…
Pulled a color chart out fast!

I whipped out some equipment
Ready, willing, feeling strong.
Applied the brilliant color
And then realized it was wrong.

That tint had covered gray hair.
Not a light one could be seen.
But the shade that had replaced it
Should have been in quarantine.

You know what? I can't do this!
I'm too angry and too old.
My hair can turn chartreuse-ish
And my love life can turn cold.

Right now I really don't care.
I'm no longer in my prime.
I'll simply keep my gray hair
And hook up with Father Time.

Face Erase

Wrinkle, wrinkle little scar
Don't take a step. Stay where you are.
Don't try to move a single inch
Though I may frown, though I may flinch.

Don't dare to think you should entrench.
Don't take a stand or try to etch
A wider, longer, deeper space
To make a line I can't erase.

I've got too many creases now.
They're all deep-furrowed on my brow.
Don't try to squeeze between those guys
Amid the lines above my eyes.

The serum-filled syringe awaits,
And jammed with Botox, smells the bait.
The jars of cream, the cleansers, masks
Are well prepared to meet their tasks.

The last defense, the strongest yet:
The age-defying laser's there
To stop, to foil, to end your threat!
So fade away. Just leave your lair.

Just go away, you little pest.
Don't try to fool technology.
I've faced the worst and beat the best.
Thank God for plastic surgery.

Gauging Aging

Fifty's the new forty,
The media's leg men shout.
But careful observations show
The numbers don't work out.

The reflection in my mirror:
The loss of tightness in my thighs,
My stretched yet still tight waistbands,
Those drooping jowls I can't disguise.

The wrinkles on my forehead,
The lines around my eyes,
The sagging of my buttocks
Predict that theory's quick demise.

Instead of gauging aging,
Why not just forget to count?
Pretend the years aren't passing,
That age isn't paramount.

Go eat and drink your heart out!
Then just lie should someone ask.
If you fear the years are showing,
Wear a cloak and buy a mask.

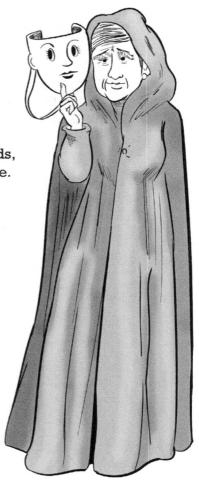

Ills, Pills And Mass Refills

I try but can't remember
When my body felt no pain.
Was it at my first reunion
Or right before the rain?

Though I do my workouts daily,
Eat with reason, play with sense,
My prescription count is rising
With a pure indifference.

It started with one bottle
To help ease a little pain.
Now their numbers keep on growing
Though the maladies remain.

I go to see my doctor
More often now than not.
And my pharmacist has told me
I'm the best friend that he's got.

Since I must still keep taking
All the potions and the pills,
My pain relief prescriptions
Are now set on "speed" refills.

My ache cup runneth over
From my head down to my toes.
It seems my four-leaf clover
Has begun to decompose.

Lube Job

I know that I am aging
From the front and from the back
When I match my chiropractor
Squeak for squeak and crack
for crack.

My body's gotten older
As the years just take their toll.
All the parts are loudly creaking
And I sense I've lost control.

My muscles always aching,
My knees and hips are blown.
All my nerve cells are awaking
While notifying every bone.

I need to add some oil,
Lube and clear out every crack,
And fix up all the weak spots
So I can have my body back.

The Pure Delight Of Cellulite

The pure delight of cellulite
Is best described in simple terms:
The years have filled my thighs with blight
A fact the lumps and bumps confirm.

Those propagating lumps of fat
Have grown and spread, are now amassed.
They've turned into a steaming vat
Of clumpy, bumpy undercast.

If I could eat a bowl of slugs
With sides of snouts and stuff that squirms
And wash them down with slime-filled mugs
Then drink a keg of deadly germs

To help me lose the undercoat
Of each and every clog-filled site,
Though knowing chances were remote,
I'd eat that crap, ditch cellulite.

Vein Terrain

Even though I still complain
To every flaming, bulging vein,
They dig in deeper, stay in place
Entrenched within their chosen
space.

They've met together, all agreed
To multiply with blinding speed,
A plan which seems to be a cinch,
As they'll soon cover every inch.

Though they are mostly varicose
The spider veins are grandiose,
A problem which I must address
Or stay a blood-lined, blue-red
mess.

VIEW FROM THE WORLD
OF TESTOSTERONE

Mr. Bright Eyes

They used to call me Bright Eyes,
My vision was so sharp.
I'd scan the whole horizon
Every ocean, hill and park.

I never asked directions,
Could envision every route.
I knew my destination,
Grabbed my coat and then set out.

So, as I clutched my car keys
And headed out the door
And hopped into my auto
As I'd always done before,

I figured I'd continue
Drive so gaily on my way,
But something soon would hit me
And completely blow my day.

As I reached an intersection
I had gone through many times,
I couldn't see so clearly
As I tried to read the signs.

That day was just the start then,
A sign of things to come.
It was clear that Mr. Bright Eyes'
Cloudless vision had succumbed.

The worst that was to happen
Would happen on the road,
When I had to bring a map in
And then couldn't read the code.

That day it finally hit me
That I couldn't see at all,
I couldn't see the large print.
It had all become so small.

The trifocals that they gave me
An optician's work of art,
Blew the mainframe of my ego.
My youthful psyche fell apart.

Say goodbye to Mr. Bright Eyes
He had his long days in the sun.
Say hello to Mr. Blight Eyes.
Appears his vision quest is done.

Compromising Position

I went in for my checkup
Like an unsuspecting lamb.
Then my doctor slapped his
glove on,
Pulled it firmly on his hand.

He smiled, said face the table,
Bend your knees and please
stay loose.
So, I did just what he told me
Without fear for my caboose.

Again I heard that glove snap
As he secured it on his hand
And then I felt his finger
As it probed my holy land.

I turned my head and queried
As best I could while in that
pose,
Said I was somewhat worried…
Could he please uncurl my
toes?

He continued with his probing
His finger moving all around,
Made some doctor-sounding noises
Nothing loud and none profound.

Now, try to get this picture:
Me with slightly bended knees,
His finger there still searching
As if looking for his keys.

I snapped and finally asked him:
"Okay, Doc, let's hear it straight!"
He smiled and then responded
"You've got a rather huge prostate."

I'd matched wits with corporate raiders
Fought with the best, met no defeat,
Kept my wife and mistress happy
And I never missed a beat.

But I swore that very moment
I'd give in no matter what
If he would just remove his finger
From my prostate-bloated butt!

Confidentmagery

Black socks are black no
question there.
With brown sandals…can't
compare.
I add plaid shorts below the
knee.
They're just so hot. That's what
"I "see.

When young guys glance
askance at me
I know it's just their jealousy.
Their eyes betray just what they
see.
They covet what is "all of me."

As I have aged with style and
grace
It seems my style has
kept the pace.
I've always known
that what I've worn
Has made most
women think of
porn…

That all those grey-haired
babes out there
Are longing for some time to
share
The stud persona that is me…
Their symbol of pure ecstasy.

So here I am within my realm
With grey-haired babes to
overwhelm.
Though most youths think my
body's shot
I know for sure that I'm just hot.

Demuscularization

I always worked the muscles
That kept my butt cheeks closed.
I clenched them tight when needed.
So my farts were not disclosed.

In concert with my South end
The muscles in my neck
Could hold a massive belch in
Keep my baritone in check.

Now, solitude was different.
With no need to hold things in
A space where I could then vent
And do it with a grin!

My throat would make the walls crack.
My rear would make things spin.
Both sending out so much flack
The ceiling crumbled in.

Again the years have played me
Slowly leading things astray
As muscle cells were let free...
Seems none had planned to stay.

They'd been used in vacant places
Where I freely let them blow
As I weakened all their braces
And naively let them go.

Now that age has taken over
And my muscle tone's awry.
My farts don't smell like clover
And my belches make me cry.

Now I make sure when I travel
It's with big crowds standing by.
So, if anything unravels
They won't know who let it fly.

Endearing Hearing

At first my lessened hearing
Was frustrating, poor and sad.
It was slowly disappearing…
Made me weary, weak, and mad.

But soon I noted changes
The more prevalent it got.
Appeared there were some ranges
It had chosen to boycott.

My wife could talk for hours,
Never stopping for a breath…
While even in my showers
She tried to worry me to death!

So my ears put up a roadblock,
Stopped all her sounds from coming near
As she kept talking nonstop
Without a word that sounded clear.

When listening to ballgames,
Friends and workmates it was fine.
It stayed within its mainframe…
Put her sound waves in decline

I love selective hearing.
It's the best part of my life.
It's made my home time more endearing.
Can't hear the nagging from my wife.

Erection Selection

If my guy's not in the mood
I can make him feel imbued.
I can take a little pill
That directs his mind uphill,

Or use a full syringe
And begin to feel the twinge
But first I must decide
How long to make the ride,

Or I can make the muscle tone
Far too much for my poor bone.
Then…to make my boy de-
crown
I'll need a pill to bring him
down.

The joy my manhood brings
Is attached with many strings
Like the lack of clear direction
At the time of my selection.

So I have to keep in mind
Just how my buddy was
designed.
That if he's showered with
affection
There'll be no need for
intercession.

Golfer's Handicap

I began my normal golf swing
Positioned straight and standing tall.
Pulled back my arms as usual,
Swung hard and missed the ball.

The pain I felt made my eyes melt.
It turned my backbone into gel.
As I sensed my body falling,
I knew things weren't going well.

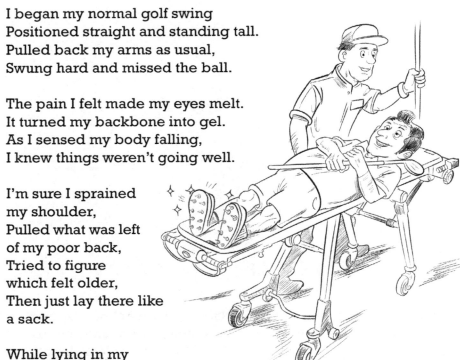

I'm sure I sprained
my shoulder,
Pulled what was left
of my poor back,
Tried to figure
which felt older,
Then just lay there like
a sack.

While lying in my
crumpled state
I entertained a thought:
I could stay there, start to vegetate
Or get back up into the cart.

I dragged myself up on my knees
Ignoring places where I hurt.
At mind's behest, pulled up the rest,
And then I wiped off all the dirt.

My mind continued working,
Said I wasn't really sore,
Said "Place the ball, go for it all.
Hit it harder than before!"

I got back into my golf stance,
Readied club, eyes on the ball,
Pulled back again then with chagrin
Felt the painful free-for-all.

My swing-through was perfection,
Club connecting with white sphere
Sending orb with clear direction…
As I dropped, I heard the cheer.

My hole in one: a deal well done,
A well-met, triumphant goal…
Though my body lay in pieces,
My mind was fresh and whole.

Despite the status of my framework
My head was in a better place
As they laid me in the ambulance,
Club in hand, smile on my face.

Hair Somewhere

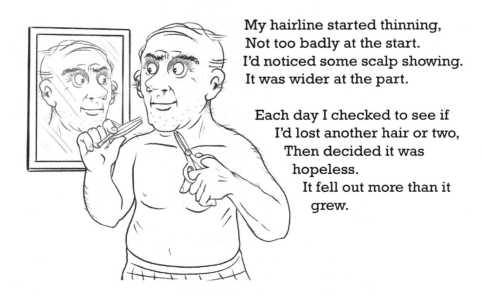

My hairline started thinning,
Not too badly at the start.
I'd noticed some scalp showing.
It was wider at the part.

Each day I checked to see if
     I'd lost another hair or two,
          Then decided it was
               hopeless.
                    It fell out more than it
                         grew.

One day as I was shaving,
Caught a glimpse of something dark.
It was peering from my nostril.
It was long and it was stark.

I asked my wife to take a moment,
Take a breath and check it out.
Had it been there…? That frightful hair
Protruding grossly from my snout?

She said: "You hadn't noticed?
Hairs have traveled from your head
To your mid-brow and your nostrils
And your ears and back instead."

When I looked back in the mirror
I saw clearly what was there.
But for my head where hair was dead,
It was growing everywhere.

My brave wife became my hero
When she gave me shield and sword:
With some scissors and strong tweezers,
Most of my ego was restored.

Jock Block

I'm so thankful for my jockstrap
Not for playing, not for sports
But to hold up what it needs to,
Keeps my stuff there in my shorts.

My favorites, the old gray ones
With elastic strings galore
Are not too tight, hold up just right
So my boys don't hit the floor.

Penultimation

The essence of my aging
Always pressing on my brain
Is effectively engaging
With my brain cells as they wane.

It creates a little vacuum
As they slowly flow away.
Thus leaving lots of spare room
For those who choose to stay.

And though it's not quite time yet
As I have a few years more???
Seems the end is not a threat yet…
Hasn't killed me while I snore.

And I can find the bathroom!
See the toilet like before
But often watch a spot bloom
As my urine hits the floor.

Still I can raise my zipper
Though that sometimes slips my mind
Until fresh air hits my dipper
And my psyche just unwinds.

Since my mindset isn't ready
With those few cells that remain.
Seems my path is clear and steady.
I just need to get a drain.

Prostate Rebate

My slowly aging husband
Was nowhere to be found.
Thought he was avoiding me.
I knew he was around.

When I checked the bathroom
And heard moaning there within
It made me stop abruptly
Quickly feeling some chagrin.

I thought it fair to wonder
What was going on inside.
Was he playing hanky panky
With his precious inborn bride?

I was getting rather angry
Knew how mad I soon would be.
I made a quick decision:
It was his inbred love or me.

So I knocked not very gently
Impatience goading my huge pride,
And entered without waiting
But then I wasn't quite so snide.

He wasn't in a love nest
With his slutty little friend.
He didn't seem too happy
And appeared a bit thin-skinned.

He was leaning rather heavily
One hand against the wall,
The other holding gently
His "lover" looking palled.

He looked so very forlorn
So frustrated, sad, subdued.
He held his badge of courage
But had met his Waterloo.

He had gone into the bathroom
As he'd always done before
To empty his full bladder
Which he could not ignore.

But when he tried to do so,
It seemed his trusty spout
Could just produce a slow drip,
Not a thing would venture out.

I think he needs a rebate.
If he paid, it was too much.
He needs a brand-new prostate
Because this one needs a crutch.

Restrooms

I rarely looked for
restrooms
Because I felt no need.
My bladder, young and
healthy,
Could hold it…
guaranteed!

I cruised through stores
and airports
With youthful, swaggered
speed.
On the road I'd go
forever
Without ever having peed.

Restaurants…delightful!
Mind centered on my meal.
I enjoyed each bite with pleasure
With, joy and "zestly" zeal,

Never once the feeling of
That pressured urge to go.
Cars and trains and buses…
Didn't matter then how slow.

All those years of freedom
Never once did it occur
That things in me were changing
Getting older than they were.

The times between my rest stops
Became shorter day by day.
My trips then took much longer
My pees were "matinee".

My bladder getting weaker
As time was passing by.
I searched for a solution
To help to keep me dry.

Then, thanks to local retail
Found the answer, so ironclad.
It could hold the liquid pressured
From my bladder to a pad.

Roadster Rehab

I left my house as usual
Keys in hand, eyes on my car,
Thinking, "Life is good I love it.
My ride's a gift. My ride's a star!"

Then I slipped into my baby
My love, my pride, my joy.
The auto that had turned me
From a man into a boy.

How trite, how very flippant
That short description sounds,
But any guy who's owned a roadster
Understands "We get around!"

I drove with sweet abandon
Felt the wind blow through my hair
Smelled the sweetness and the freedom
Felt the freshness of the air.

I pulled into my same space
Cut the engine, grabbed my stuff.
I pulled the door's bright handle
Thinking "Oh, this baby's tough!"

But when I tried to get up
I knew everything was wrong.
I needed something extra,
Something helpful, something strong.

I'd had a sports-car spasm.
Couldn't move without great pain.
My legs were barely mobile
And seemed out of their domain.

While I waited for a winch truck
My mind was grinding out the gears.
I'd have to change direction
To fit my bulging middle years.

Thoughts Of Wonderlust

Alas, so many years ago
When just a naïve, virile youth
So laced with vigor, oats to sow,
I only saw hormone-raged truth.

The waves of passion made their way
From mind, to heart, to body sound.
Embraces filled both night and day,
So rapture-filled, a breeding ground.

To neck, to grasp, to squeeze, to grope . . .
To touch, to feel, to sense, to taste . . .
To dream then knead with liquid soap . . .
Those were the days I didn't waste.

As time progressed, my pace then slowed.
I yearned for less and lost my zest.
I chased my girls by area code
My goal to simply keep abreast.

My dates now done before their start,
My urge for sex is now a bust.
I've lost my edge, played out my
part
And live my life in
Wonderlust.

MIDDLE AGE ROMANCE: THE REALM OF HEAVY BREATHING

Appointment

We've set up an appointment
The first day of every week
So we can get some nooky
Do the nasty cheek to cheek.

That's when I plan my errands
Form a mental, weekly route.
Think of what I need to do
On those days when I go out.

He likes to hear Bolero.
I like to check my nails.
He's on the straight and narrow.
I'm thinking of the sales.

But once my engine's going
Revved up by his manliness,
I forget what I was thinking
And join in with some finesse.

By the time we both are finished
My week is planned, and more.
Plus, I'm sated, smiling, happy
And halfway through the door.

Belly Dancing

As we dance we hear the lyrics,
Music streaming through the air,
  And we hold each other closely
  Both so glib, both unaware.

  Our chests are bonded tightly
  Cheeks together, breath on hold,
  We glide so very lightly
  Oh, so gently and controlled.

  We move in subtle motion
  Thoughts on hold in sheer
    delight,
    Feeling pure and deep
  devotion
      As we sashay through the
      night.

Unaware that time has triumphed
Blasting litheness on its way,
Sending chests down to our middles
Making muscles go astray.

Observers, quite objective,
Can see our love is pure,
But with a clear perspective
View our love now as mature.

The closeness that existed
In our breasts as we embraced
Still lives and breathes between us
But it meets up at our waists.

Middle Age Mating

Middle Age Dating leads
To Middle Age Mating
Where some upper lip hair
Doesn't stop a brief affair.

It could be a simple start
Though one of you might fart
When the dinner date is done
And you're really having fun.

When that extra bit of paunch
Doesn't seem to stop the launch
Of a quick, one night affair
With someone who has no hair,

And, the climax that you seek
Might be just a wee bit weak.
As you stop and realize
At your age, you compromise.

It seems that Middle Age dating
Can be quite a bit deflating
But it sure beats the opposite
Of your remaining celibate!

Over The Hill Romantic

I'm an over the hill romantic.
Who is just a wee bit frantic.
It seems that my sexual self
Has passed the date called "shelf."

I'm an over the hill romantic
Who's eternally, madly, lovesick
With relationships sad and so few
And a liaison far overdue.

But, for me there remains some hope
That I can still find some horny dope
Who's as bad off and moldy as me
Who'll be happy to get it for free.

Wrecking Necking

When I felt the urge to kiss
My older, sweet new miss
I tried to raise my arm,
Which set off my pain alarm.

As my shoulder said, "No way!
You have to change your play!"
I moved in to close the space
For a sweet, unplanned embrace.

I tried a hug so void of grace
I quickly lost my place.
That's when our panicked eyes revealed
Our fear as it congealed.

We forgot we had old breath
Since it was past our fiftieth,
And that hormonal excess sweat
Made our lips a sloppy wet.

But, again we moved in close
And then began to diagnose
That the way to feed this urge
Was to back off instead of merge.

Our simultaneous release
Gave us both a quiet peace
So when our eyes could finally meet
We agreed to no defeat.

The lust that stoked our body heat
Fueled our urgent need to eat.
So hand in hand we walked away
To find the closest huge buffet.

AND SO, IT GOES, AND GOES, AND GOES . . .

Rite Of Passage

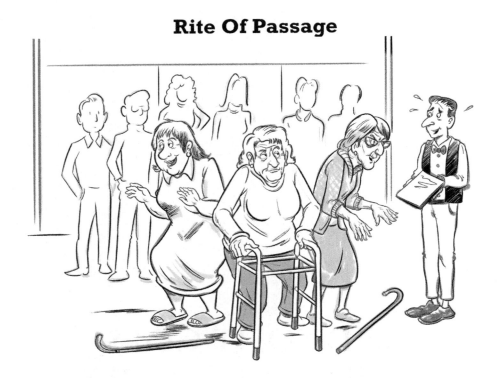

We love to go to dinner
Finding places close nearby.
Early Bird…the most important
Are the ones that qualify.

We walk right to a table
Ignoring the long line
And no one dares to stop us
With our walkers, canes and wine.

We seat ourselves with clatter
As our canes drop to the floor
While all the waiting patrons
Stare with shock from the front door.

Not waiting for a server
Shouting "waiter!" right away
We smile so very sweetly...
Reeling in our prey.

Their trepidation, inching slowly
To our table we ignore
And pounce on them so quickly...
Their knees barely miss the floor.

We say that we are ready
And want to order right away.
With pen in hand they're waiting
Knowing this is NOT child's play.

With sweat effusing quickly
They shake and wait with fear
As we ask about each item...
Sometimes they shed a tear.

We eat our meals quite slowly
Still annoying those in line
And never even notice
As our burps and farts entwine.

And then, when we have finished
Having very slowly grazed
We mill through those still waiting
And all of them seem dazed.

Working On It

I started out quite perfect
Staying steady for awhile
But passing years have shown me
There's a drastic change of style.

The hips are somewhat broader
Joints have gotten dry and weak.
Appears my face has fallen
And I'm somewhere past my peak.

Though my body parts are going
At a far-too-rapid pace
And my age is clearly showing,
There's still a bit of grace.

It seems I've gained some
knowledge,
Bits and pieces on my way.
I am smarter and I'm wiser
Learning more the less I say.

I'm still a work in progress
Praying daily for less pain
But soaking up the moments
In the parts that don't complain.

Reversion

I thought I had my pants on
When I walked out my front door.
I saw my neighbors waving
As they'd always done before.

But none of them were smiling
And they seemed a bit perplexed,
Questions on their faces
As they all began to text.

They made some frantic gestures
With lots of angst all aimed at me.
Now perplexed and in a quandary,
Couldn't think what it could be.

Then I saw them pointing downward
Faces filled with disbelief.
So I followed all their fingers
To my baggy, pure white briefs.

With redness moving upward
From my neck then through
my face,
I back-stepped through the doorway
As best I could in my disgrace.

Maturation process finished,
With my life now in reverse,
The next step seems apparent:
Find a patient, strong-assed nurse.

Entre Deux Ages

There's a list of words and phrases.
Some refer to middle age.
One of the most intriguing
Is the title of this page.

It means between two ages
Perhaps a simple thought.
But I'm scratching for survival
And I'm feeling quite distraught.

Though the phrase is esoteric
And it's meant to sound alright
It's haughty and it's faulty,
Thus, it makes me feel uptight.

Yes, it's between two ages
    With a timeframe of its own.
    It's that frame I've found myself in—
    A consistent combat zone.

    Appears as I've been aging
      Childhood habits have returned.
      The things the years had taught me
      Have been steadily unlearned.

    Since this slowly-aging process
      Makes my mindset want to scream
      I'll skip the entre deux days
      Going forward with full steam.

    So I plan to go out smiling.
      With my mind now in this phase.
      I'll leave others to explain things
      When I check out in a daze.

So, I Am?

Not to seem too morbid,
But I've got to tell the truth.
There's not a single thread left
Of my virile, happy youth.

I'm living somewhere else now
With people my own age
But I'd be so thrilled and happy
To turn back the latest page.

This place is really lovely,
The scent of flowers in the air
So many smiling faces
But it's odd how much they stare.

Most of them are walking
Using canes with ample skill.
There are others speeding past them
Doing wheelies for the thrill.

So, this is just what happens
As I glide past middle age...
My thoughts are still adjusting
Trying hard to re-engage.

It's fine if I'm not all here
Didn't figure that I'd be
Just traversing through this playground
With a brain that's absentee.

AN AFTERTHOUGHT...

EPILOGUE:
ARE WE THERE YET?

Glossary

absentee, *n.* brain cells. lots of brain cells.

aging, *n.* what men over 50 call women over 30.

aging, *n.* what women over 50 call men over 70.

bending, *v.* precursor to bent

bent, *n.* the inability to straighten caused by bending (see **bending).**

blemish, *n.* what a zit is called after the age of 50.

boobs, *n.* those perky little things men call pacifiers (see also **gravity, women).**

butt, *n.* the pert little area that used to hold up your pants but now just holds up the people trying to get around it.

calorie, *n.* the measure of energy for food taken in but no longer expended in bodies over the age of 50.

cellulite, n. the lumpy sludge lurking under one's unwitting skin conspiring to make its move to the hips, butt and thighs.

chest, *n.* the part of a man's anatomy which, if pumped, all women regardless of age find yummy (see also **gravity, men).**

children, *n.* offspring who bring delight until they are old enough to seek revenge.

collagen, *n.* that which is absent in the bodies of the middle age melted.

common sense, *n.* must have missed that meeting.

constipation, *n.* when younger, a minor blockage easily cleared by consuming a Philly Cheesesteak.

constipation, *n.* when older, a major blockage caused by eating a Philly Cheesesteak.

crepe, *n.* the stand-in for collagen.

dating, *v.* to keep company with, to tolerate, to seek a moment of bliss with the bald, the bloated, the physically-corrugated opposite sex.

deadline, *n.* didn't know it was this long…would have brought a bottle.

devotion, *n.* the first emotional attachment one feels for one's significant other; the aftermath of middle age segueing into a lust for food, a good bed and no back talk.

diaper, *n.* porta-potty for seniors.

digestion, *n.* assimilation of food ingested occurring in anyone under the age of 50 (for those over 50, see **indigestion**).

divergent, *n.* paths which synapses take to screw with our brains.

divorce, *n.* result of an unhappy husband seeking a woman 20 to 30 years younger than current model with a deliriously happy ex-wife having rid herself of aforementioned baggage and receiving a financial windfall as a bonus.

exercise, *n.* unknown

exigency, *n.* where's the bathroom?!!

fart, *n.* (women) fastest way to end a bad date

fart, *n.* (men) no disclaimer...just comes with the package

gravity, *n.* (women) natural occurrence wherein once perky boobs make friends with the belly button.

gravity, *n.* (men) natural occurrence wherein once firm chests become boobs.

gray hair, *n.* when found anywhere on the anatomy, causes seizures.

hair, *n.* that which used to exist on the head but then migrates to its happy places in the ears, nose and back.

hearing, *n.* selective device used by males to mute bitching females.

hesitate, *v.* what the last shred of the conscious mind does before its unconscious body continues to do something stupid

imagination, *n.* she/he wants me soooo much!

indigestion, *n.* the digestive track's act of revenge in response to too much digestion during the body's first 50 years of ingesting.

instincts, *n.* you might not want to go in there.

irony. *n.* aging is such a warm, fuzzy feeling.

iterating, *v.* thinking. thinking. not thinking. thinking, not thinking. thinking.

jock, *n.* young stud bucket of a guy; accessory used by stud buckets; sling which holds up what used to be the reason for a stud bucket being called a stud bucket.

knees, *n.* the creaky, nonfunctioning, painful area lying between the thighs and shins.

maturation, n. (women) mini boob stage segueing into filled bra stage wherein teen boys find something to fondle other than themselves.

maturation, *n.* (men) growth stage wherein the thing they found attached to their baby selves which had made life worth living took second place to boobs

melt, *v.* the process during which the body collapses from lack of collagen, sinew and bone mass

memory, *v.* put on underwear, don't fart in public, restroom means potty not naptime place.

menopause, *n.* that which gives men pause to question, touch, bother or otherwise enter the space of a woman experiencing same.

middle age, *n.* point at which life begins to end as we know it.

mind, *v.* do I mind? no, no. not at all!

movement, *n.* what our bowels dream of

muscle, *n.* the sinuous mass which, when bulked, attracts most women regardless of age but sadly seems to dissipate exponentially in the 50 and older lot.

obituaries, *n.* check every morning. If you're not there, go have your coffee.

paradox, *n.* after all that we're still here?

pedantic, *adj.* the word used to excuse the obnoxious, opinionated, and annoying comments we enjoy making and getting away with due to our age.

phlegm, *n.* the yuck we used to love to hack up and spit as kids, but now hack up because we will choke to death if we don't.

pills, *n.* the cause of bankruptcy in the latter years.

PMS, *n.* a monthly occurrence in females from puberty until menopause, better known among singles as "preferred mode of suffering" as opposed to pregnancy.

porcine, *adj.* the kindest word used to describe a fat old fart.

prostate, *n..* If exceptionally large, may morph into the following:

prostrate, *n.* position men find themselves in after learning they have an enlarged prostate.

protuberances, *n.* regrettable extensions of the nose and ears resultant from years of growth so far beyond the pubescent stage that growth charts caved in.

recruits, *n.* category of women, usually under the age of 30, sought by most men over the age of 50.

reiterating, *v.* re-thinking while iterating thinking.

reparations, *n.* the ignored, unappreciated efforts made by the conscious mind to repair bodily damage which occurred while in its unconscious state.

repeat, *v.* the stomach's way of saying "I told you so!"

restroom, *n.* so misleading . . . when you're done, you have to get up and leave.

reunion, *n.* function to be actively avoided if physicality has declined and/or increased exponentially since the previous get-together.

reversion, *n.* the U-turn moment wherein the road to maturity ends and the lapse into mindlessness begins.

sex, *n.* rings a bell . . . just not sure which one.

sexy, *adj.* the delusional image that middle agers prefer to think they exude.

stomach, *n.* that which used to be flat, but now, not so much.

toot, *n.* latest in propulsion methods for the over-the-hill.

undercast, *n.* the thickly cobblestoned, fat-filled area just below the epidermis predominantly situated in the upper thighs and arms.

veins, *n.* the map from knees to ankles ending where shoes should be placed.

vision, *n.* that which, as it becomes more blurred, makes hot dates such hot dates.

wings, *n.* sagging, fleshy, collagen-needy area of the arms located between the armpits and elbows.

wonderlust, *n.* state of mind regarding urges to which one has forgotten how to respond.

wrinkles, *n.* see lines, see valleys, see schisms, see what you see but know they have friends who love to rent free.

wrinkle, *v.* what happens to one's skin when one sees a wrinkle (see above: wrinkles, *n.*)

About The Author

Janet lives in Norfolk, Virginia with her husband, Steve. She is not very interesting. However, while nail filing," grass growing watching", paper shredding junk mail, and various other pursuits, she has managed to put together some thoughts culminating with this collection of nonsense.

Janet was Salutatorian of her graduating class at Newport News High School, Newport News, Virginia. From there she went to Temple University in Philadelphia, Pennsylvania where in her first six weeks her thirst for knowledge led her to make Dean's List knowing she would have an extended deadline of 11pm vs. 9 pm for Freshmen. She majored in Business Administration with a minor in Law. That education culminated into a secretarial/administrative position leading into an Assistant Block Trading position at Legg Mason. Her business career was not stellar, but taught her how to navigate all the bullshit.

Thankfully, now all she does is write bullshit.

Made in the USA
Las Vegas, NV
15 April 2022